THE STARS

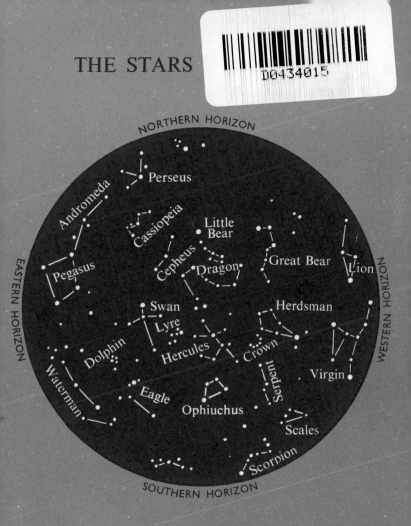

May 2 a.m.

June midnight

July 10 p.m.

August 8 p.m.

Series 536

The heavens at night provide one of the most beautiful spectacles of nature. The Moon, the bright planets, the patterns of the stars are all lovely to look at, and your pleasure is increased if you can recognize the various objects and if you know where to look for them at different times.

This book will help you to recognize some of the stars and planets; it tells you some fascinating facts about the Moon, the Milky Way, galaxies, comets and 'shooting stars', and will fill you with wonder at the great mystery of our universe.

The NIGHT SKY

by MARY T. BRÜCK, Ph.D.
(Royal Observatory, Edinburgh)
with illustrations by ROBERT AYTON

Publishers: Wills & Hepworth Ltd., Loughborough
First published 1965 © *Printed in England*

The Starry Sky

The heavens at night provide one of the most beautiful spectacles of nature. The Moon, the bright planets, the patterns of the stars are all lovely to look at. Your pleasure is increased if you can recognize the various objects, and if you know where to look for them at different times.

Much can be seen without the help of any instrument, but, of course, it is fun to have a telescope. A small one, or a pair of binoculars, is all you want for the beginning.

Practise using your telescope in daytime by setting it on distant hills or buildings. When you actually view the stars, you will then need only to push the eye-piece a little further into the tube to make the picture clear and sharp. Keep the telescope steady, and start sighting the object across the top of the tube before you look through the eye-piece.

If you are using a star chart at night, have a dim torch ready; do not dazzle your eyes once they have become accustomed to the darkness.

4

7214 0104 X

The Earth and the Solar System

The Earth from which we view the world around us, is a large ball about eight thousand miles across. Its surface is wrinkled with mountains and valleys and more than two-thirds of it is covered with water. Enclosing it all is a blanket of air called the atmosphere.

There is nothing special about the Earth. It is one of a family of nine planets, all going round the Sun, each at its own pace in its own track. The ones nearer to the Sun move faster than the outer ones. Mercury, the innermost, goes round in only three months, while Pluto, the most distant, three thousand six hundred million miles away, circuits in about two hundred and fifty years. The Earth, ninety three million miles from the Sun, takes one year to go once round its orbit.

To the naked eye the planets look just like stars, but we can tell that they are different from the way they move. While real stars keep to the same patterns in the sky, planets follow their own courses among them, and by observing them for a few weeks one can distinguish them quite readily.

The Motion of the Heavens

If the Earth stood still, every star in the sky would always be found in the same place. But the Earth moves not only round the Sun once a year but—what is more noticeable—spins on its axis once a day. As a result of the spinning, the whole sky, Sun, Moon and stars, appear to move in the opposite direction.

The Sun, going from east to west each day, is the most obvious sign of the daily rotation of the Earth. During the night the stars, too, move in the same way. If at night you put a camera in an open window, facing the starry sky, and leave it with the shutter open for an hour or two, you would find when you developed the film that each star had left a trail showing how it had moved in the meantime.

The spin of the Earth marks our days and is used to keep time. A sundial keeps time by the Sun, but it is more accurate to measure time by the stars, and this is in fact how the world's clocks are regulated.

The Sun

When the Sun is shining, you must *never* look directly at it, as you might seriously damage your eyes. However, you *can* get a view of its disc if you let its light pass through a pin-hole pricked in a piece of cardboard, and let it fall on to another card or a wall behind. The speckled patterns of light and shade under leafy trees in summer are made up, too, of coins of light, pictures of the Sun which are produced by the gaps between the leaves.

The Sun is a ball of hot vapour, and its diameter is about one hundred times that of the Earth. In volume it is big enough to hold a million bodies like the Earth. The bright face has a temperature of six thousand degrees centigrade, and the inside even more. So intensely hot are its central regions that nuclear energy is produced there naturally, just as it is artificially in a hydrogen bomb explosion. Hydrogen is the most plentiful material in the Sun and is a very economical fuel for the supply of light and heat. The Sun has been shining for many thousand million years, and yet it has enough hydrogen left to keep it shining for an even longer time to come.

The Sun's Face

It is even more dangerous to use a telescope for looking at the Sun. Instead, you should follow the same method as with the pin-hole—let the Sun's light pass through the telescope on to a screen behind. By moving the eye-end in and out you can get a clear picture of the Sun projected on the screen.

A large picture of the Sun often shows up sunspots, dark blots on the Sun's face which do not last long, but appear and disappear usually in a matter of days or, at most, weeks. They indicate storms in the gases at the Sun's surface, and they are particularly plentiful every eleven years. The next crop is due in 1969. On rare occasions spots become large enough to be plainly seen without the help of any instrument.

All stars, if you could look at them at close quarters, would look similar to the Sun. Some stars are bigger, some smaller, but all are hot balls of gas which shine by nuclear energy in their interiors.

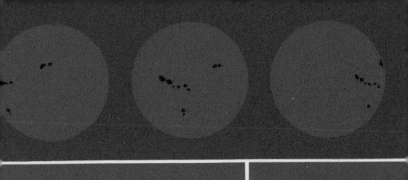

Above: Illustration shows movement of sunspots across the Sun's face over nine days.

Left: Close-up of sunspot group.

Below: How to project the Sun through a telescope.

The Moon

Our nearest neighbour in space is the Moon. It is two hundred and forty thousand miles away and has already been reached by rockets from the Earth. Its whole surface is only about the size of Africa, and it is completely dry land.

The Moon shines by reflecting some of the Sun's light falling on it. It goes round the Earth once a month, and while it does, we see more or less of its sunny side; its phase changes from crescent to full Moon to crescent again.

A new Moon is always seen in the west, after sunset, with its bright crescent lying towards the Sun. Sometimes along with the bright new Moon we notice a dim full Moon. This is the 'earthshine'—that means sunlight reflected from our bright Earth and shining on the dark part of the Moon, just as moonlight lights the Earth at night.

As the month goes by, the Moon moves eastwards away from the Sun, and, at the end of the month, we see the last thin crescent at morning, in the east, near the rising Sun.

The Lunar Landscape

The Moon shows up as a particularly interesting object in a telescope. The best time to look is when it is about half full, because at this phase the slanting rays of the Sun illuminate the mountains along the straight edge down the middle of the Moon, throwing long shadows on the ground and making the landscape stand out clearly.

There are mountain ranges there, about the same height as mountains on the Earth, and wide, smooth plains (called seas) which look less bright than the surrounding rough country, because they reflect less light. It is these which cause the pattern of the 'man in the Moon'. Most interesting of all are the craters of circular shape which are dotted all over the Moon's face, many of which are believed to have been formed by large meteors crashing there in the distant past.

Neither air nor water exists on the Moon. There is no rain, wind or weather there—and, of course, no life. It is a dead, silent world. The Moon, too, keeps the same face turned towards the Earth, which explains why the same 'man' is always there.

SEA OF COLD

PLATO

SEA OF RAINS

ARISTARCHUS

APENNINES

SEA OF SERENITY

OCEAN OF STORMS

COPERNICUS

SEA OF VAPOURS

SEA OF TRANQUILLITY

SEA OF CONFLICTS

SEA OF HUMORS

SEA OF NECTAR

SEA OF FERTILITY

TYCHO

LEIBNITZ MOUNTAINS

Morning and Evening Stars

When you see what looks like a brilliant star in the west or south-west in the evening, shining all alone in the sky before the other stars appear, it is almost certainly the planet Venus. When it is not an evening star, it is a morning star in the east or south-east before sunrise. It alternates between evening and morning, spending seven or eight months in each, with only a short absence in between.

Venus is about the same size as our Earth, and is next to us in the Sun's system. Being nearer the Sun, it is hotter, and is covered all over with a coat of thick white clouds. Through a telescope, Venus shows changing phases like the Moon, according as it moves round the Sun.

If you have a clear view of the western horizon on a spring evening, you may spot the tiny planet Mercury. It is almost impossible to see it at other times. It is actually not much bigger than the Moon, and, like the Moon, is an airless, lifeless globe.

VENUS

MERCURY

Comparative sizes

EARTH   VENUS

MERCURY   MOON

VENUS

Jupiter

A very brilliant planet seen at night is sure to be Jupiter. It looks like Venus, but, while Venus can only be a morning or evening star, Jupiter can appear at any hour from sunset to dawn and can take up any position from east through south to west.

Though five hundred million miles away from the Sun, Jupiter is extremely bright on account of its enormous size, as big in bulk as all the other planets put together. Far away from the Sun's heat, it is locked in a crust of thousands of miles of solid ice, and is covered with an atmosphere of heavy poisonous gases.

In a telescope or binoculars, Jupiter looks like a bright sixpence with four little dots of light nearby. These are Jupiter's main moons—there are altogether twelve—and, like our own Moon, they go round the planet continually. If you make a drawing of the positions of the moons you will see how much they have moved when you observe them again the following night.

Mars

Though not always conspicuous, the planet Mars can be recognized from its strikingly red colour. Its brightness varies greatly; every two years its journey round the Sun brings it unusually close to the Earth, and in those years (1965, 1967, etc.) it is particularly noticeable.

Viewed through a telescope, Mars is a disappointing sight. This is because it is small, hardly more than half the size of the Earth. Its orange-red colour is due to the sandy deserts which cover most of its surface. White caps can be seen near the poles of the axis round which Mars rotates, which remind us of the snowy polar regions on our own Earth. On Mars, however, it is only hoar-frost, and this melts away quickly during the summer. Like Earth, Mars has its four seasons; when it is winter on one hemisphere, it is summer on the other just as on our own planet.

Water is scarce on Mars; so is oxygen, the part of the air which we need for life. There may well be living things on Mars, but they can only be simple plants like mosses, which do not need much water or oxygen to keep them alive.

Mars seen through a telescope (south pole at top)
Above: Winter   Below: Summer in its southern hemisphere.

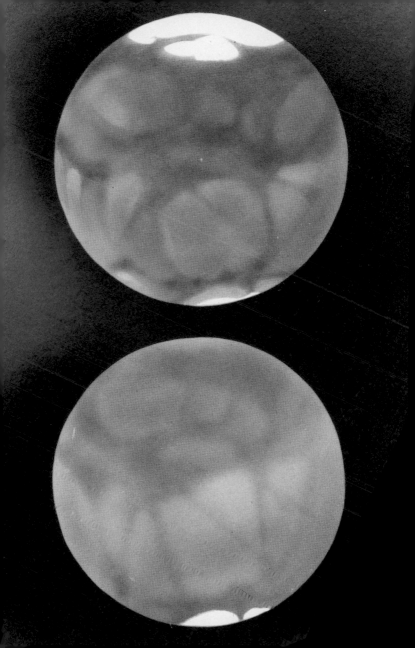

Saturn

Saturn can easily be mistaken for an ordinary star. It is whitish and no brighter than many of the bright stars in the sky. Fortunately, at present, and for a number of years to come, Saturn will be in a part of the sky where there are few bright stars, which makes it easier to recognize.

Seen from the Sun, Saturn lies beyond Jupiter and is, like Jupiter, another large and icy planet. Through a telescope it looks remarkably beautiful, having bright hoops or rings circling around it. These rings are made of millions of ice-covered pebbles which move round Saturn like so many million moons. Apart from its rings, Saturn owns nine proper moons of which the largest, Titan, can be seen with a small telescope.

Beyond Saturn are three smaller planets, Uranus, eptune and Pluto. They are even colder than Saturn, g further away from the Sun.

SATURN

URANUS NEPTUNE PLUTO

THE FISHES

P'

1967

SOUTH

Comets

Apart from planets, the Sun has another family of quite a different kind—the comets. They, too, move round the Sun in regular tracks or orbits, but, whereas planets move in paths which are very nearly circular, a comet's orbit is long and narrow, so that it spends the greater part of its time in the dark distant regions of the solar system. Only for a very short part of each circuit is a comet near the Sun.

Unlike planets, comets are not solid bodies, but loose swarms of small icy particles. When near the Sun, the ice evaporates in the Sun's heat; the comet begins to glow and becomes visible.

There are probably many millions of comets in the solar system, though very few of them become illuminated and only an occasional one is bright enough to be seen with the naked eye. It can be a spectacular sight— a bright head with a feathery tail sweeping upwards from The tail is made of gas blown out of the comet by Sun's rays. Once the comet moves away from the he tail disperses and the comet fades away into s once more.

Meteors and Meteorites

When we speak of shooting stars we mean meteors, which are not stars at all, but tiny scraps of matter which come in from outer space and get burned up in our atmosphere as they tear through.

Larger meteors or fireballs sometimes leave a trail like a jet plane's which may last for many minutes. If you happened to be in the vicinity of a fireball, you would hear a clap like thunder as the meteor rushed through the air. Occasionally, pieces of burned material can be picked up on the ground; they are meteorites, lumps of rough stone or iron. Every museum has samples of such meteorites.

On a dark, clear night you ought to count about one shooting star every five or ten minutes. At certain times of the year you will see many more. This happens when the Earth meets the remains of some bygone comet, whose dust may cause the appearance of whole swarms of meteors. Good times for meteor swarms are July 29th to August 18th, November 14th to 19th, and December 8th to 15th.

The Constellations

Certain patterns of bright stars, called constellations, have beautiful names which date back to ancient times when they were named after heroes of legend, or after beasts or birds which their shapes resemble. The names of constellations are useful for specifying regions of the sky, like names of countries on the Earth. Many individual stars have names, too, like towns within the countries.

Everyone knows the constellation of the Great Bear, sometimes called the Plough or Dipper, which is always in the sky. Of the seven bright stars, the two front ones are called the pointers because they indicate the location of the Pole star, at a distance about five times the distance between the two stars themselves.

The Pole star stands almost directly above the Earth's North Pole, and is therefore due north at all times; other stars appear to travel round the Pole in circles. In northern countries, stars in the region of the Great Bear never set; they are visible all through the year at all times of night.

CASSIOPEIA

CEPHEUS

DRAGON

Pole S

GREAT BEA

LIT

NORTHERN

The Sky Near Orion

The most splendid constellations appear in winter in the southern half of the sky, and are so conspicuous that even city dwellers cannot fail to see them. The brightest is Orion, the Great Hunter. The three bright stars in a row mark his belt, from which hangs his sword made up of fainter stars. Orion is followed by his dogs; here you cannot miss Sirius, the Dogstar, which is the very brightest star in the sky and also one of the nearest to us.

The distances of stars are so great that it would be senseless to express them in the units used in our everyday life. Instead, distances in the universe are reckoned in light-years, a light-year being the distance which light travels in one year. Since the speed of light is one hundred and eighty-six thousand miles a second, a light-year amounts to almost six million million miles!

The distance separating neighbouring stars is roughly 'ew light-years. Sirius is nine light-years away—a distance, considering that most stars are hundreds n thousands of light-years away.

CHARIOTEER ← *Capella*

PERSEU

TWINS

Pleiade

LITTLE DOG

OR

Sirius

GREA

SOUTHER

The Spring Sky

As winter passes, Orion and its neighbouring constellations drift out of sight and others come into view. Summer approaches with the appearance of the Lion. On late spring evenings this constellation stands in the south and right in front of us. The head and forelegs of the Lion look like a sickle, with a brilliant star called Regulus at the bottom.

East of the Lion is the Virgin, with its bright star Spica. Another conspicuous star is Arcturus, the brightest in the constellation of the Herdsman. First trace the Great Bear and, following the direction of its tail downwards, you will find it leads to Arcturus.

As you look around the sky, you will notice distinct differences in colour between stars. Arcturus has a yellow tinge, Spica and Regulus are bluish-white. The differences in colour arise from differences in temperature; the blue ones are hotter than those with yellow hues.

HERDSMAN

Arcturus

LION

VIRGIN

Regulu

Spica

SOUTHERN SKY, S

Telescopes

Individual stars are generally disappointing sights when viewed through a telescope. Even the nearest of them are so distant that they look no bigger than bright dots, however large the instrument. For observing the stars, the telescope is not intended as a magnifier, but as a light collector. A telescope of, say, six inches in diameter, has a light-receiving area five hundred times greater than a human eye; stars look that much brighter when seen through it. Stars which are too faint to be seen at all with the naked eye, can show up through a telescope, and the larger the telescope the more stars can be seen.

Starlight collected by large modern telescopes is often studied with special equipment, such as a photometer which measures brightness, or a spectroscope which separates the light into its various rainbow colours or its spectrum. The spectrum tells us what materials a star is made of, and also how hot it is. All stars are similar to the Sun, though they vary considerably in size, temperature and light-giving power.

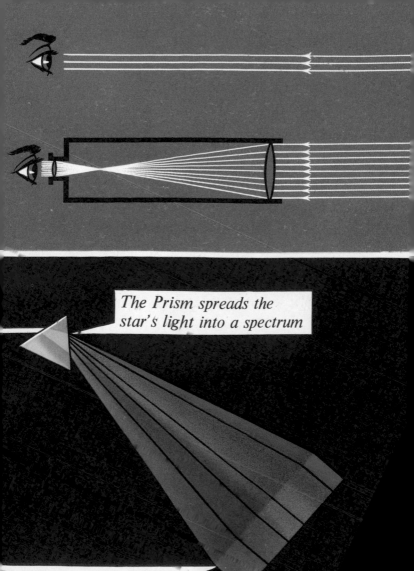

The Prism spreads the star's light into a spectrum

Details of a star's spectrum tell what the star is made of

Double Stars

The sky contains many stars which, though appearing no different from their neighbours when seen with the naked eye, turn out to be double when viewed through the telescope. In these stars the two members revolve around each other continually, just as the Earth revolves around the Sun. The star Beta Cygni, in the constellation of the Swan, is a double star which can easily be seen as a pair with a small telescope. The bright star Castor in the constellation of the Twins is also double; so is the Pole Star.

Often the two stars in a double star are so close together that one crosses in front of the other periodically, obscuring some of the light of the one behind. This naturally makes the combined star look fainter for a time. An example of this type of star is Algol, a moderately bright star in the constellation Perseus. Here the two stars revolve around each other once in only three days, and for five hours out of every three days Algol is temporarily only a third of its usual brightness.

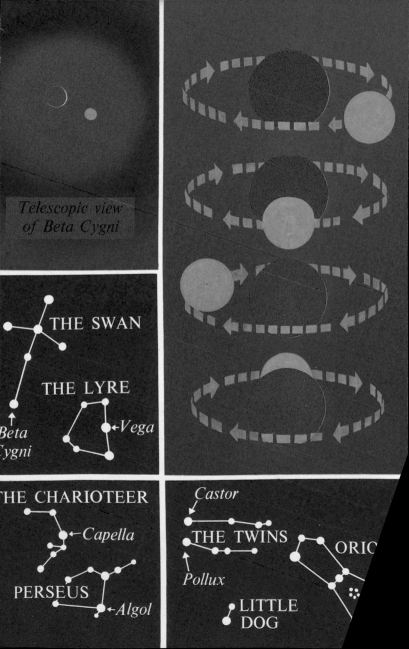

Telescopic view of Beta Cygni

THE SWAN

THE LYRE

Beta
Cygni

Vega

THE CHARIOTEER

Capella

PERSEUS

Algol

Castor

THE TWINS

ORIC

Pollux

LITTLE
DOG

The Orion Nebula

On a clear night, it is easy to spot in the sword of Orion a pale hazy patch among the stars. This is the Great Nebula in Orion, and is well worth looking at through binoculars.

The word 'nebula' means a cloud, and this nebula is a real cloud of dust and gas, as far away from us as the Orion stars themselves. It is the type of cloud out of which all stars were originally formed, by condensing somewhat like water drops out of steam. The oldest stars we know condensed as long ago as fifteen thousand million years, but stars are forming still, and within the Orion Nebula we observe some very young, recently formed stars. Whole families of stars are usually formed together out of one large cloud. An example of such a family is the pretty star cluster of the Pleiades, not far from Orion.

According as a star condenses it becomes increasingly hot until it can tap its sources of nuclear energy. A big problem in astronomy to-day is to trace the life history of stars from the moment they condense until they have used up all their energy.

THE BULL

Pleiades

ORION

Nebula

The Milky Way

On summer and autumn nights the Milky Way stretches overhead roughly from east to west like a huge bridge spanning the sky. It is a pale white track, wider and brighter in some places than in others.

With a telescope or binoculars you will see that the Milky Way is made up of countless stars packed closely together. It is like looking into a forest, where the trees are so thick that you see only a mass of wood. That is what the Milky Way is—a forest of stars.

The Milky Way forest is called the Galaxy. The Sun, near which we live, is just one of the stars of that enormous group, as are all the individual stars which we see elsewhere in the sky.

Also in the Galaxy are vast quantities of clouds, both bright (similar to the nebula in Orion) and dark. The western half of the Milky Way, which we see opposite, divides in two like the prongs of a fork. This is not a real split; it is where dark clouds cover up our view of the stars in the central part.

The Galaxy

It is easy to guess that the Milky Way does not end at the horizon, but encircles the whole sky like a giant wheel. The other half, which is seen from the southern hemisphere, is brighter and more striking than our northern part.

To build up a complete picture of the Galaxy, photographs are taken through special telescopes of the stars and nebulae in the various parts of the Milky Way. Radio telescopes are used, too, which can pick up radio waves from invisible gas between the stars.

When all the information is pieced together, it appears that there are about one hundred thousand million stars in the Galaxy, and about the same amount of material in the form of gas and dust. The whole is arranged in the shape of a wheel, one hundred thousand light-years in diameter, and about two thousand light-years thick. Our home within the Galaxy is not in the middle of the group, but about half-way between the centre and the rim as shown by the cross in the illustration. This explains why the star forest looks denser in certain directions than in others.

The Andromeda Nebula

The name "Andromeda" is well known, not because it is a particularly conspicuous constellation, but because it contains the famous Andromeda Nebula, the largest and most distant object which our eyes can see. During autumn and winter Andromeda is in the sky, and on a really dark evening in November or December you ought to be able to locate the nebula almost overhead, a dim, hazy blob, which looks larger through a telescope or binoculars.

In spite of being called a 'nebula', this object is not a cloud like the Orion Nebula. It is not even a member of our Milky Way. It is an enormous collection of stars and star clouds, right beyond our Galaxy in space, at a distance of two million light-years. It is hard to imagine such a distance, from which light spends two million years travelling before it reaches our eyes. The Andromeda Nebula contains as many stars as our own Galaxy, and more. In fact, it is another galaxy quite separate from ours.

Andromeda is not the only outside galaxy. It is simply the nearest of millions of similar ones, scattered through distant space up to, and beyond, the limits of vision of our largest telescopes.

CASSIOPEIA

Nebula

ANDROMEDA

PEGASUS

THE RAM

Large Astronomical Instruments

When it comes to studying distant regions of space, really large instruments are needed. The largest telescope in the world to-day is the two hundred-inch reflector in California, which collects light with a mirror, sixteen-and-a-half feet in diameter. Even with this enormous instrument, the farthest galaxies are not *seen;* they only show up on photographs after many hours' exposure.

Large radio telescopes are used for the same purpose. Stars and galaxies give out radio waves, as well as ordinary light, and radio telescopes are instruments which collect and register these waves coming in from space. The radio telescope at Jodrell Bank, in England, the world's largest, uses a metal network saucer two hundred and fifty feet wide to collect the radio waves.

Stars also give out a certain amount of ultra-violet light and x-rays, but these very powerful rays are cut off by the air in our atmosphere. To pick them up, instruments are flown above the atmosphere in rockets or satellites, and very soon large telescopes in orbit will be helping to solve the problems of the universe.

Above: Jodrell Bank Radio Telescope.   Below: The two hundred inch telescope at Mount Palomar, California.

The Universe

As large telescopes probe further and further into space, more and more galaxies are discovered. Far from being the only one, the Milky Way is one of millions, which fill space out to some ten thousand million light-years, the farthest distance which our present-day telescopes can reach.

The galaxies form the bricks out of which the large-scale universe is built, and they are separated by distances of a few million light-years. But the distances are not fixed. The galaxies all seem to move apart, outwards from each other, as if the whole universe were stretching like a balloon which is being inflated.

Why do they spread out in this way? Did they all start in one great huddle some thousands of millions of years ago, before being blown apart and scattering as we now see them? Or is there another explanation for the "expansion of the universe", as it is called? We do not know. This remains one of the great mysteries of the universe.

THE STARS IN AUTUMN

August 2 a.m.   October 10 p.m.

September midnight   November 8 p.m.